Achieving Life Balance

Taking Action for a Better Life

Sam R. Lloyd and Tina Berthelot

A Crisp Fifty-Minute™ Series Book

This Fifty-Minute™ Book is designed to be "read with a pencil." It is an excellent workbook for self-study as well as classroom learning. All material is copyright-protected and cannot be duplicated without permission from the publisher. *Therefore, be sure to order a copy for every training participant by contacting:*

THOMSON

™

COURSE TECHNOLOGY

1-800-442-7477 ◆ 25 Thomson Place, Boston, MA ◆ www.courseilt.com

Achieving Life Balance

Taking Action for a Better Life

Sam R. Lloyd and Tina Berthelot

CREDITS:

Senior Editor:	**Debbie Woodbury**
Editor:	**Ann Gosch**
Assistant Editor:	**Genevieve McDermott**
Production Manager:	**Denise Powers**
Design:	**Nicole Phillips**
Production Artist:	**Rich Lehl**
Design Adaptation:	**Daniel Quackenbush**

For more information contact:

Course Technology
25 Thomson Place
Boston, MA 02210

Or find us on the Web at **www.courseilt.com**

For permission to use material from this text or product, submit a request online at: www.thomsonrights.com

Any additional questions about permissions can be submitted by e-mail to: thomsonrights@thomson.com

Trademarks

Crisp Fifty-Minute Series is a trademark of Course Technology.

Some of the product names and company names used in this book have been used for identification purposes only and may be trademarks or registered trademarks of their respective manufacturers and sellers.

Disclaimer

Course Technology reserves the right to revise this publication and make changes from time to time in its content without notice.

ISBN 0-619-25906-X
Library of Congress Catalog Card Number 2004114290
Printed in Canada

Learning Objectives for

ACHIEVING LIFE BALANCE

The learning objectives for *Achieving Life Balance* are listed below. They have been developed to guide you, the reader, to the core issues covered in this book.

The objectives of this book are:

❏ 1) To explore the meaning of life balance and in what ways your own life may not be balanced the way you would like

❏ 2) To explain goal setting and creating action plans to meet your goals

❏ 3) To help you discover your psychological drivers and reprogram them for more positive results

❏ 4) To present strategies for managing your time according to your values

❏ 5) To demonstrate effective ways to manage your relationships with others

Assessing Your Progress

In addition to the learning objectives above, Course Technology has developed a Crisp Series **assessment** that covers the fundamental information presented in this book. A 25-item, multiple-choice and true/false questionnaire allows the reader to evaluate his or her comprehension of the subject matter. To buy the assessment and answer key, go to www.courseilt.com and search on the book title or via the assessment format, or call 1-800-442-7477.

Assessments should not be used in any employee-selection process.

About the Authors

Sam R. Lloyd, M.B.A., is the founder and president of SuccessSystems Inc., an international training and development consulting firm based in Boulder, Colorado. For more than 30 years, Sam has worked with people in organizations of all types and sizes to improve their personal and interpersonal effectiveness.

Before starting SuccessSystems, Sam was the director of management development programs for the Cox School of Business at Southern Methodist University and earlier was the assistant dean for continuing education in the School of Business Administration at the University of Missouri-St. Louis.

He is the author of *Developing Positive Assertiveness, Self-Empowerment, Accountability: Managing for Maximum Results*, and *Leading Teams: The Skills for Success*.

Tina Berthelot, M.Th., is the owner and vice president of SuccessSystems Inc. Besides designing and delivering training programs, the company provides personal coaching services for individuals. Tina joined SuccessSystems in 1983 after working as an investment broker and in human resources for International Harvester.

She is the co-author of *Self-Empowerment* and is active in the Colorado Human Resources Association, the Boulder Area Human Resources Association, and the USA Transactional Analysis Association.

Sam and Tina are husband and wife. More information about them and their company is available at www.trainingforsuccess.com.

Preface

In recent years more and more people have become concerned about achieving life balance. Employee surveys have revealed that the majority of employees rank life balance concerns as one of the most important factors when considering employment or advancement opportunities or whether to stay with their current employer.

Men and women now seem to want a life in which their work and family responsibilities are more balanced than was true for past generations. Whether you are single or married, young or mature, a parent or not, this book has been created to help you evaluate your own life balance and to give you tools and techniques for achieving the kind of balance you desire.

To achieve your desired life balance will require making some changes, and you are most likely to accomplish this by doing all of the exercises in the book. Just reading the content will not produce the changes—you will need to take action. And the exercises are designed to help you do that.

You will be most successful if you go through this book more than once! Changing your current life patterns will take some work and it will be easier to just continue doing what you have always done. Rereading the book and redoing the exercises will help you make the changes you decide to make and integrate those changes into a new and better way to live your life.

We wish you success with your quest!

Sam Lloyd   Tina Berthelot

Table of Contents

What Is Balance

for You?

Defining Life Balance

What is the ideal life balance? Only you can answer this question because it is your values, goals, dreams, and desires that determine what will be most satisfactory for you. You will be happiest when you live your life in the manner that best meets your needs.

Right now you may be doing what many people do—living your life in a manner determined only partly by your own wishes and partly by what others expect or demand of you. You may be living out a script that was chosen in early childhood and influenced by messages you heard (or thought you heard) from parents, grandparents, and other significant adults.

You can take charge, rewrite this script, and change the way you are living by getting in touch with your real wants, needs, values, and priorities; setting some goals; and taking the action steps required to accomplish your goals.

Survey: The Meaning of Life Balance

For a better idea of what people think about life balance, let's look at the results of a survey. The respondents were male and female; some married, some not; some were parents; some were young adults, others were middle-aged, and some were approaching retirement. Here is what a few had to say about the meaning of life balance:

"Life balance means that I can enjoy the best of both worlds without guilt."

"Spending the amount of time on each aspect of your life according to how important that aspect is to you. In other words, not 'wasting' time on insignificant (to you) aspects that take time away from doing things that are more meaningful (to you)."

"Life balance means having the desired balance of work and life responsibilities. This differs for each individual, and for me includes having the time to make a positive impact in my personal life (being able to do the things I want to do—travel, relax, spend time with family members and friends, comfortable income, etc.) and still make a profound impact at work. If I am away from the job too often, it may affect my job performance. Conversely, if I am unable to achieve or attempt to achieve my personal goals outside of the office, that may also affect my job performance. It is a very tricky balance and needs to have deliberate and direct attention. It will not simply take care of itself."

Write your own definition of *life balance*: _____

_____

_____

Identifying How You Spend Your Time

The starting point for improving your life balance is getting a clear picture of your current life situation to help you see what you want to change. Think about these aspects of life and evaluate how much of your time each week you are devoting to each. There are 168 hours in a week.

WORK: If you have a job, career, or some source of income that requires your active involvement and energy, how much time do you devote to this part of your life each week? ____ hours

PLAY: The opposite of work is play (recreation, fun, leisure, pleasure-seeking activity). How much time do you devote to this part of your life each week? ____ hours

FAMILY: Whether you are closely involved or only minimally involved with your immediate family (spouse, children, parents, grandparents, other relatives, and in-laws), how much time do you devote to this part of your life each week? ____ hours

SOCIAL: This category refers to your other relationships outside of work (friends, acquaintances, neighbors, club members, etc.). How much time do you spend with them each week? ____ hours

HEALTH/FITNESS: How much time do you devote to maintaining your health (exercise, treatment, physical therapy, etc.) each week? ____ hours

FINANCIAL: Besides the work you do to produce an income, how much time each week do you devote to financial planning, budgeting, investing, paying bills, or other things related to your financial requirements? ____ hours

BEING/PERSONAL GROWTH: This category refers to those things you do to meet your autonomy needs, to help you feel fulfilled, to help you feel good about yourself, or to satisfy your desire for meaning in your life. For some, these are intellectual pursuits, education, writing, seminars, and the like. For others this includes meditation, walks in the woods, visits to art galleries, or religious pursuits. For still others, this category involves psychotherapy, support groups, or personal challenges to test your limits or learn something about yourself. How much time do your devote to this part of your life each week? ____ hours

Charting Your Life Balance

Now that you have thought about each of the life balance components and estimated how much time you devote to each one, create a pie chart below by dividing the circle into segments representing the amount of time you spend in each pursuit. This will help you see how your life is arranged currently.

My Typical Week

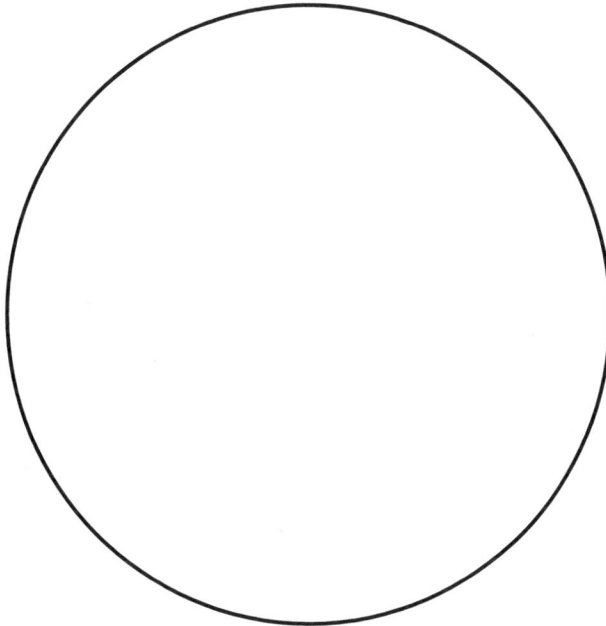

As you look at this pie chart, you can see how much of your time and energy is being directed to each segment of your life. Do you like what you see? If you do, that is great news! You seem to be doing a good job of balancing your time and effort in a way that suits your values and preferences.

If you do not like what you see, you may now have a better idea of where your life is out of balance—where you are devoting more time and energy in ways that do not give you the satisfaction you deserve—and where you would like to spend more time.

Chart Your Ideal Life Balance

If you would rather have a different life balance than the one you charted previously, create another pie chart in the following circle to represent what you would prefer.

My New Life Balance

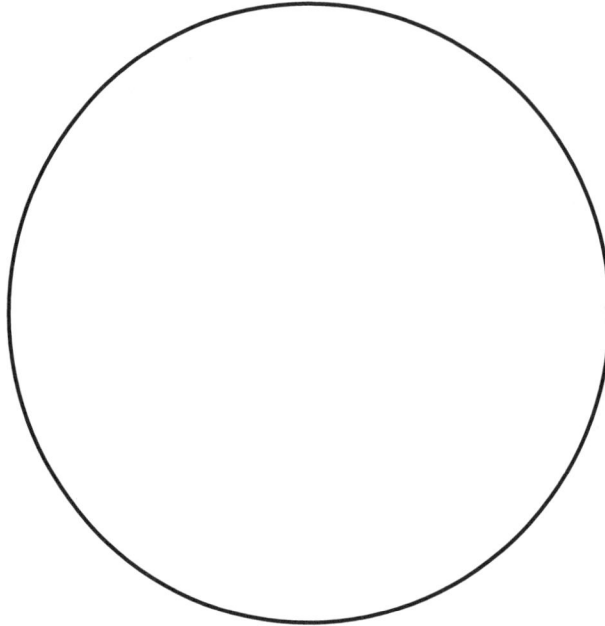

The pie chart exercise is only one way to evaluate whether you are content with your current life balance. The exercise on the next page is another way to see how well you are doing in achieving the life balance you want.

Assessing Your Values

Are you living in line with the values that you hold dear? It is important to have a clear understanding of the relative importance of your values to help you assess your current life balance and decide where you might want to make changes.

Making decisions and taking actions necessary to satisfy your more important values as much as possible means you are living your daily life with your higher-priority values as your guide. If you rank some values at a lower priority, this does not mean that you are ignoring them. It means only that they play a lesser role in how you live your life. When you do have to make choices that involve your values, you will be more likely to protect your higher-priority values rather than low-priority ones.

Aligning Your Life with Your Values

Once you identify which values are of high, medium, or low priority for you, then you can assess how you are structuring your time and activities and where you are devoting your energy. Where are you getting each of your values satisfied? Is it in the home or at work? Maybe a particular value is being satisfied 70% through your work and 30% at home or in other parts of your life.

Thinking about each value and where that value is playing a prominent and satisfying role in your life may help you recognize why you spend the amount of time and energy in some parts of your life that you do. It may also help you see where to make changes.

If one of your high-priority values, for example, is helping others and you discover that the primary place (80%) that you are able to live out this value is in the home (nonwork) part of your life—but you are working outside the home 55 hours a week—you might decide to make some changes. You could restructure your time to have more hours available for helping others. Or you might decide to change your job to give you more opportunities to help others as part of your work.

Another way to consider your values and priorities is to answer honestly this question for each of your high-priority values: "Am I really living my life according to this value?"

For example, many people place a high priority on love, affection, family, and friends. But when they answer the above question honestly, they become aware that their current life balance is devoted to other values! They have little time available for being with family or friends and they are devoting very little energy to this aspect compared to other parts of their lives. It can be uncomfortable and even sad to realize that you have structured your life in a manner that does not allow for satisfying one of your most important values.

Are You Living in Line with Your Values?

Completing this step-by-step exercise will help you think about your values and the relative importance of each. As a result, you may see a need to make changes to live more in line with your priorities.

Step 1: In the table on the next page, divide the 18 value categories into three equal groups. In the column labeled "Priority," write A for your most important values, B for those that are of medium importance, and C for those that are least important. Be sure you have six in each group. (Note: You may have other values that you want to add to this list and assign an A, B, or C priority to them.)

Step 2: Assess where you are getting each of your values satisfied. For each one, place a checkmark (✔) in the box labeled "Work" or "Home." Or write a percentage in the box for how much of this value is being satisfied at work vs. home.

Step 3: For each of your A values and if you like, your B values, answer the following question honestly: *Am I really living my life according to this value?* Write "yes" or "no" in the "Living" column.

Value	Priority	Work	Home	Living
1. Achievement, accomplishment, doing				
2. Advancement, promotions, moving up				
3. Adventure, challenge, taking chances for payoffs				
4. Affection, love, relationships, friends, family				
5. Influence with others, feeling in control				
6. Financial security, adequate income, little or no debt				
7. Freedom, independence, choosing your own path				
8. Involvement, belonging, being included				
9. Inner harmony, peace of mind, low stress				
10. Health, physical fitness				
11. Fun, play, recreation, good times				
12. Learning, reading, intellectual stimulation				
13. Helping others, contributing, giving of yourself				
14. Status, prestige, recognition, fame				
15. Creativity, self-expression				
16. Spirituality, religion, meaning of life				
17. Personal growth, self-esteem, self-actualization				
18. Wealth, riches, material possessions				

If this exercise helps you realize that you are not quite living according to your own important values, please do not disapprove of yourself. Few people manage to live consistently by their own value system. Everyone has room for improvement, and that is what this book is about.

You may want to ask the significant other people in your life to complete this values and priorities exercise. After they have done so, compare your similarities and differences. The conversations about your respective values and priorities may provide a new understanding of conflicts within your relationships.

Scrutinizing Your Schedule

Are you spending your time in line with your values? Examining this question is yet another way to become more aware of the balance in your current lifestyle. Think about what you do during a week, estimate the time devoted to each activity, and determine to which of your values each one is related.

Start by making a list of all of the things you do. (The common activities already listed on this chart will help you get started. Feel free to cross out any that do not apply to you.)

Things I do during a week:	Hours	Value
1. Travel to and from work		
2. Work		
3. Housekeeping (cleaning, repairs, laundry, etc.)		
4. Transport children to school/activities		
5. Meal preparation		
6. Entertaining		
7. Volunteer work		
8.		
9.		
10.		
11.		
12.		
13.		
14.		
15.		

Estimate the time in hours that you devote each week to what is on your list and write your estimate in the "Hours" column. (Be sure the total does not exceed 168—that's all the hours there are in one week!)

Now think about which of your values each of the activities on your list supports. In the "Value" column, write the number corresponding to those values from the previous exercise.

When you have done this exercise, then you can examine how much time and energy you are investing in activities related to different values. Are you spending the most time on your A, and possibly B, values? Are you spending too much time on C values?

If all of this seems like a lot of work, remember that only you determine how satisfying your life is for you. Only you make the choices about how you use your time and energy. These exercises are designed to help you honestly evaluate your current life balance and see where you want and need to make new choices to help you achieve the most satisfying balance. No one else can do it for you. If you will do this work, your reward will be the satisfaction gained from the improved balance and the reduced stress when you achieve your balance goals.

CASE STUDY: Commuting Takes Its Toll

Cameron was aware of a growing dissatisfaction with his life and the accompanying stress but could not identify the underlying cause. He recognized his frequent irritability and the negative impact his mood was having on his relationship with his wife and their two young children.

After months of stress, bouts of anger followed by guilt, and physical symptoms such as headaches, sleeplessness, and gastric distress, Cameron decided that something had to change. His employer had an employee assistance program and he decided to see a counselor.

After a few visits with the counselor, Cameron identified that his stress was tied to his growing dissatisfaction with his job. He enjoyed his work but disliked the commute. He had to leave home at 6:45 each morning to make it to work by 8 and usually did not get home until almost 7 in the evening. Cameron had little time with his children during the week and felt pressured to devote a lot of his weekend time to them. He was aware that household duties, friendships, and private time with his wife were suffering because he was reserving weekend time for the children. This awareness added to his stress.

With his counselor's assistance, Cameron thought seriously about his values and priorities and concluded that his life was out of balance and that he needed to make some changes. After talking with his wife, his manager, and the human resources people in his organization, he negotiated a flextime arrangement that allowed him to work from home two days a week. This allowed him to drive his children to school on those days, and he and the children took on the responsibility for preparing meals together on those evenings. He also spent fun time with the children on those evenings.

These changes allowed Cameron and his wife to use their weekend time differently, too, because Cameron no longer felt pressured to spend most of his weekend with the children. Soon Cameron was no longer emotionally and physically distressed. He was enjoying his life more. His work quality improved too.

Because Cameron identified the source of his discomfort and decided to make changes in line with his values and priorities, he created a better life balance and became more satisfied overall.

Setting Goals and Action Plans

Understanding Goal Setting

Now that you have examined your values and priorities, and your current and desired life balance, it is time to translate this thinking into goals.

What is a goal? Write your answer below.

_____

_____

As simple as this sounds—*a result you want to accomplish*—it is important that you understand clearly the significance of what a goal is. It is not a plan and it is not an activity. It is the *outcome* that results from carrying out a plan and doing the planned activities or tasks.

Many people think that making a to-do list is goal-setting. Not true! Setting goals means doing some serious thinking about the results you want to achieve at some point in the future—what you hope to have when you have done all of the to-dos.

It is a good idea to write down your goals and post them as a visual reminder of what you are planning to accomplish. Some goals can take a while to accomplish and having the goal posted where you see it regularly helps you stay on track.

A goal is simply a statement of what you plan to achieve. It is a result you want to accomplish.

Writing Goals Using the SMARTS Criteria

You will be more successful in accomplishing your goals if you write them according to six basic criteria. It may help you think of them as the *SMARTS* criteria for good goals. The acronym is formed by the first letter of each criterion, as follows:

S **imple and Specific**—State your goal in uncomplicated language and make sure it is a specific objective. A goal that is flowery and full of big words may sound impressive but it is easier to remember and to communicate to others if it is worded in plain, simple language. A goal that is vague or ambiguous is unlikely to be accomplished. A specific target is more likely to be reached.

M **easurable**—Think about and decide how you will measure the accomplishment of your goal. If a result cannot be measured, there is no way to know whether the goal has been accomplished. Ideally, use numbers somehow to measure the goal.

A **chievable**—It is fine to make a goal challenging but make certain that it can be achieved. If you define a goal that is unattainable, then you are setting yourself up for disappointment and frustration when you fail. Even though most of us rise to a challenge, do yourself a favor and make sure that the goal is realistic to ensure that you will actually accomplish it.

R **esult**—A goal was defined as a statement of a planned outcome. It is important that you write down a *result*, not a task. Tasks are the steps taken toward the eventual accomplishment of the goal. The goal is the result you have achieved when all the tasks have been done.

T **ime**—To keep focused on the accomplishment, you must include a time limit or time frame in your goal statement. Someone once defined a goal as a "wish with a time limit"! Without a time limit, the hoped-for outcome too easily remains a wish or a dream. Having a time frame helps you continue working toward the result until you have achieved it.

S **hare**—Telling others what you plan to achieve helps you accomplish your goal for several reasons. Most of our achievements involve other people in some way. Others can help by doing some of the tasks, by providing moral support, by contributing ideas, by taking on some of your other responsibilities so you can focus on your goal, or by checking on your progress. Telling others also increases your commitment. It is easy to give up when your goal is a secret. But when you have made it known to others, you will want to continue working on it until you accomplish it. You have put yourself on the line by sharing your objective with others.

EVALUATE THESE GOAL STATEMENTS

Even though the SMARTS criteria sound simple, most people find that doing a good job of defining goals takes work. Sometimes you may have to rewrite a goal several times before it finally satisfies these criteria.

To help you learn to write high-quality goals, read the following statements and decide which ones satisfy the six criteria for effective goals. Check (✔) the box of each statement that satisfies all six criteria. For those that do not, write on the line below the statement how it fails.

❑ I will spend more time with my children.

_____

❑ I will lose 12 pounds during the next four months.

_____

❑ By the end of next year I will be able to have conversations in Spanish.

_____

❑ I will retire comfortably by age 60.

_____

❑ I will work on improving my relationship with my spouse during the next year.

_____

❑ I will have three new friends by the end of the summer.

_____

Compare your answers with the authors' responses in the Appendix.

Setting Goals to Fulfill Your Values

Even though the idea of goal setting seems simple, actually doing it takes practice before you learn to do it well. Get some practice now. Look back at your high-priority values and select one or two. Use the spaces below to write some goals related to your values.

Remember, you are defining the outcome you want to achieve and not the action steps you will take. It is best to think about the action steps only after you have developed goals that meet the SMARTS criteria.

My VALUE: _____

GOAL: _____

_____

_____

My VALUE: _____

GOAL: _____

_____

_____

My VALUE: _____

GOAL: _____

_____

_____

Often people do not realize when they have failed to write a goal that meets the SMARTS criteria. How can you be sure that you have succeeded? Share the information about goals and the SMARTS criteria with a friend or colleague, and then ask that person to read and evaluate your goal statements. The feedback you receive may help you improve any statements that do not satisfy all of the criteria. In so doing, you also will be sharing your goals with at least one other person.

CASE STUDY: A New Career Path

Stacy was a successful accountant for a large, national public accounting firm. In addition to having a B.S. degree in accounting, she was nearing the completion of an M.B.A. degree. During her final semester she became aware that she was asking herself if she really wanted to continue working as an accountant.

She often felt exhausted from long trips involving traveling by air, carrying luggage, sleeping in hotels, eating in restaurants, spending lonely hours in her hotel room doing paperwork, checking e-mail messages, returning phone calls, and watching television reruns. Stacy began to long for a lifestyle that would allow her to be home with her friends. It seemed to her that the only time she saw her friends was on the few weekends that she could go out with them to bars or other activities. She wished she could just spend a quiet evening with her friends during the week.

Stacy remembered reading a book about goal setting and charting your own course, and she looked through her bookcases until she found the book. After reading it again, she devoted an evening to doing the goal-setting exercises. She became even more aware that she needed to make some changes. Her primary goal became discovering a new career path that would allow her to be home most of the time. She set a time limit of eight months to accomplish that goal. She needed five months to complete her M.B.A. degree, which she decided was important to give her maximum flexibility with whatever new career goal she developed.

By the time she finished her degree, Stacy had investigated several new career options and decided to seek employment in a smaller company in the human relations function. She had become aware that the accounting and financial area did not interest her as much as it once had, and she wanted to work more with the people aspect of organizations. She wanted a smaller organization because she thought that would help her feel more involved and part of a team.

After clarifying her goals, Stacy was able to find a new job as a human relations specialist with a 200-person company that manufactured medical instruments. She was not required to travel, she was able to be with her old friends more often, and she made new friends at work. She not only was pleased about being able to be home most of the time, but she also discovered that she really enjoyed her new work.

Defining Action Steps for Achieving Your Goals

Having a well-defined goal is an important starting point to achieving a goal. Without a goal that meets the SMARTS criteria, we often feel that our time and effort are not producing the results we really want. Still, having a good goal is no guarantee of success. You also need to take action steps toward that goal.

It is true that sometimes when we have a clearly defined goal planted in our subconscious, we tend to make it happen even without a conscious plan. But you cannot count on that happening. That is why the best way to ensure that you accomplish your goals is to identify the action steps required to achieve your desired outcome.

Tap into Your Creativity

Coming up with action steps may be easier for you if you get your creative juices flowing before you start thinking about how to accomplish a goal. Here are some ideas about how to do that:

➤ **Get relaxed**. Do some vigorous exercise, take a hot shower or bath, listen to relaxing music, light a scented candle, do some deep breathing. This lowers your stress level and helps you to activate the creative side of your brain.

➤ **Have some fun**. Watch a comedy routine on TV, play some lighthearted games, laugh, and giggle. This gets you into the childlike part of your personality, which is where your creativity is centered.

➤ **Choose an unconventional place to do your thinking**. Lie on your stomach on the floor, sit on a cushion on the floor or in the middle of your bed, or go to a park where children are playing. If you sit at your desk, your creativity may be stifled because you associate your desk with work or other "adult" things.

Brainstorming for Action Steps

Brainstorming has proven to produce high-quality ideas for solving problems or achieving goals. Ideally, a small group of people (six seems to be an effective number) agrees to work together to generate ideas. To make the most effective use of this technique, the group agrees to follow the rules of brainstorming:

> ➤ All ideas are okay and desired (no matter how silly, impractical, costly, etc.)—The more ideas generated, the better the chance of ending up with effective ones

> ➤ No evaluation or judgment of ideas is allowed—Negative comments about suggested ideas will quickly stifle creativity and result in individuals' withholding ideas

> ➤ Everyone contributes—It is okay to pass if you do not have an idea at the moment but it is important for all to participate to help create synergy (the phenomenon of one person's idea sparking an idea in someone else)

> ➤ It is okay to "piggyback" on others' ideas—Your idea does not have to be completely original; it can be an extension or a different version of an idea that was already suggested

> ➤ Every idea offered is written down—Later you come back to the list to evaluate and select those that are most usable and likely to help accomplish the goal

Brainstorming is fun and exciting and produces an amazing number of good ideas. It always produces more ideas than one person would have developed on his own and in a very short time. Usually it also results in some ideas that you simply would not have thought of. This is because different people have different experiences, knowledge, and thinking processes. By combining efforts you benefit from these differences.

Other Ideas for Developing Action Steps

A side benefit of brainstorming comes from sharing your goal with the others in your session. This can result in their continuing to support and help you achieve the goal even beyond the session itself. But you can also share your goal with others (friend, co-worker, boss, spouse, mentor, etc.) outside of a brainstorming session. Ask each person for two or three ideas about how to accomplish the goal.

Or try the following ideas for developing action steps toward meeting your goals:

➤ Read biographies, self-help books, and magazine articles about how others have achieved similar goals.

➤ Participate in an e-mail discussion group and post your goal statement. Ask for ideas about how to achieve it. Others seem to enjoy offering ideas if you just ask.

➤ Keep a notepad and pencil by your bed so you can jot down ideas that develop while you are falling asleep or dreaming—some of our best ideas come this way.

ACTION STEP PRACTICE SESSION

Use one of the goals you wrote earlier to practice thinking up action steps. In the spaces below, write down all of the ideas you can think of. They do not have to be in the order you would do them. Just start to think of things you could do that would help you achieve your goal and write them down. All you need is the basic idea. You can always come back later and develop the idea more completely. Keep going rather than stopping to evaluate your idea. It is better to think of lots of ideas to spark your creativity and get a productive flow of ideas started.

Action Steps

Ask Others

Now share your goal with a few other people. Tell them why you want to accomplish the goal. Share your ideas from your action steps list and ask them for more ideas. This way you are likely to gain additional high-quality ideas that will help you develop a plan for accomplishing your goal.

Avoid Judging Others' Ideas

When you ask others for their ideas about how to accomplish your goal, listen carefully to what they suggest and write down all of the ideas offered without evaluating or commenting on those ideas.

Many people have a habit of responding to others' suggestions by saying something such as, "Yes, but that costs too much." The "yes, but" response tells others that you disagree with their idea or that you think their idea is not very good. This discourages them from helping you. The "yes, but" response also invites them to argue with you and to defend their idea, which can lead to an unpleasant encounter.

Developing an Action Plan

After you have considered all of the ideas for accomplishing your goal and have decided which ones are good ideas that can be implemented, it is time to develop your action plan and start achieving. Remember that your goal must have a time limit or timeline. Your action plan also must consist of a schedule of action steps. Some of your action steps can be implemented concurrently, and others can be done only after earlier steps have been accomplished. The order in which to carry out your action steps is important.

Sample Action Plan

What follows is an example of how you might draft your action plan to achieve the goal of losing 18 pounds. This will give you an idea of how to draft your own plans to meet your goals.

Goal: I will lose 18 pounds within the next six months to help me be healthy and fit.

Action Steps:

Eat smaller portions

Eat lower-fat and lower-calorie foods

Eat more fruits and vegetables

Buy a high-quality pedometer

Walk at least 5,000 steps each day

Increase muscle mass by doing weight training two to three times a week

Stop buying snack foods

Eat at fast-food restaurants less often (once a week or less)

Limit alcohol consumption to an average of one drink a day

Get an exercise buddy

Join a health club

Buy exercise equipment for home

Plan a reward for success

Get more attention and affection from others

Learn how to measure muscle/fat ratio

Action Plan:

➤ Week 1: Buy a good pedometer, buy groceries (allow time to read labels and choose healthful foods), check out available health clubs, talk with friends who belong to health clubs to find out what they like and dislike about their clubs, wear my pedometer every day to measure how many steps I take, buy a journal for recording what I eat each day, how many steps I take, and how much I weigh.

➤ Week 2: Check out exercise equipment for home, decide if I will join health club, buy my own equipment or do both and implement the decision, invite one or two friends to be exercise buddies and work out an exercise schedule (walking, hiking, biking, weights), decide what my reward will be after six months and losing 15 pounds or more.

➤ Week 3: Continue healthful eating, adjust exercise schedule and walking to make sure I do enough to continue losing weight and increasing muscle mass, evaluate progress (should weigh two pounds less by now!), make sure I am getting attention/affection from others so I won't use food for strokes.

➤ Week 4: Evaluate my patterns and progress (am I eating right, exercising enough, getting my attention needs met; do I feel good about myself and what I am doing?). Continue eating healthfully, exercising, checking my weight (should weigh three pounds less now). Put a big sign on my bathroom mirror to celebrate my success so far!

- _____
- _____
- _____

➤ Week 26: Measure my body fat and muscle mass. Celebrate my success by buying a new outfit to fit my new, lean body and having my friends applaud and whistle when I wear my new clothes for them!

Is it important to have a written action plan for each goal? Yes! You are most likely to accomplish your goals when you have invested the time and effort in figuring out action steps and organizing them into an action plan with a timeline. Otherwise it is easy to slip back into old patterns. An action plan helps you stay focused on the new directions and goals to help you achieve a more satisfactory life balance.

Take the time now to write your own action plan using the goal and action steps you drafted in the previous practice session exercise. You can apply this procedure (goal, action steps, action plan) to every goal you want to accomplish.

Are you beginning to think that all of this planning is taking a lot of time that you could be using for getting things done? Be patient! The time invested in thinking and planning will pay off with better results. There is an old saying that is very true: Proper Planning Prevents Poor Performance. Think of this planning as *investing* time rather than "spending" time. The process is an investment in your eventual success and satisfying life balance.

P A R T 3

Managing
Your Self

Understanding "Life Script"

One of the biggest barriers to a balanced life can be ourselves, as the following examples illustrate:

➤ Many managers are so busy making sure every little thing is done exactly right that they end up spending 65 to 70 hours a week at work. The problem is that working this many hours each week does not fit their idea of a balanced life. Their spouse and children complain about how little they are home.

➤ There is the mother who always volunteers to drive the neighborhood children to and from soccer practice, bakes cookies for the school bake sale, prepares dinner parties for her husband's boss, and does all of this while working full-time outside the home. When you ask her what she wants for herself, she really has no answer other than making sure her family is happy. She admits to feeling guilty about thinking about herself very much. She also says that her doctor has prescribed medication to help her deal with stress and sleep better because she worries about her husband and children so much.

There are many more examples of how people make choices that result in an unbalanced life. A primary influence in such choices is early decisions we made during our formative years as children.

Childhood Influences

In our formative years we are trying to find the answers to important questions. Who am I? Who are all of these other people? What am I supposed to do? Where do I fit in?

As young children we are searching for a sense of identity and trying to sort out what life is all about. Most of us do not think about these questions at the conscious level. We are doing this subconsciously and the answers are not given to us by others. We come to our own conclusions based on our life experiences—what we see and hear; our failures and successes; our pleasures, disappointments, and fears; and our interpretations and guesses.

We eventually decide who we are, where we are going, how we will get there, and many other conclusions. We do all of this when we are young, uneducated, and inexperienced. And these decisions guide our choices and actions throughout our lives. The concept of life script is a way of talking about these early decisions.

Like a movie or play script, our life script is a story, and we are the central player in the story. Usually there are parts of our life script that are positive and life enriching and parts that are not. Unfortunately, many people do not write a very happy script for themselves! Fortunately, it is possible to become aware that your script is not one you want to follow through your whole life. And it is possible to rewrite your script. This can be a critical part of your achieving life balance.

Uncovering Your Own Life Script

Our life scripts typically remain at the unconscious level but they influence our daily decisions, how we perceive our choices, and how we live our lives. Becoming aware of your own unconscious plan can help you decide if you want to do a little rewriting of your life script.

One way to do this is through favorite fairy tales. Did your parents and others read fairy tales to you when you were little? What was your favorite?

_____

Why did you like this one better than all of the others?

_____

_____

What lessons did you learn from this tale or what decisions did you make?

_____

_____

In the following accounts, this book's co-authors identify their own favorite fairy tales and how these tales helped write their life scripts.

In the story of the Three Little Pigs, I identified with the third little pig, the one who built his house with bricks so the big, bad wolf could not blow it down as he had the other pigs' straw and stick homes. I learned to plan and be cautious and prepared to make sure not to get hurt or caught by surprise. Not surprisingly, I became an adult who plans, considers alternatives before making decisions, does not take unnecessary risks, and so on. I also have had to learn to be more trusting of others.

I did not have a favorite fairy tale but I have vivid memories of a children's television program called "Winky Dink." Each day the viewers were asked to help save Winky Dink from some perilous situation by drawing on a colored plastic sheet placed over the television screen. I would draw a bridge, or a rope, or a horse for Winky Dink to escape from danger! I played a similar role in my family by protecting my brother or mother when my father was angry or by helping other family members when they were having a problem. This compulsion to rescue others is still a pattern that I fight. I have to work to avoid putting others' needs first at the expense of my own needs and priorities.

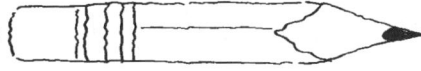

YOU COULD BE IN THEATER!

Here is another interesting technique for becoming aware of your own life script:

Close your eyes and imagine yourself on a theater stage behind the closed curtains. Continue to imagine yourself at center stage while the house lights dim and the curtain opens. See yourself on the stage as the spotlight focuses on you. What do you do next? Imagine yourself from the opening moment of the play to the closing moment. Watch the story unfold and be aware of the role you play.

This works best with your eyes closed imagining as vividly as you can each scene from the opening curtain to the conclusion of the performance. Give it a try and write the notes about your play on the lines that follow:

_____

_____

_____

_____

_____

_____

In the following account, one of this book's co-authors identifies life changes made as a result of doing this exercise:

I did this exercise at about age 35 and became aware of a "play" that called for a life of solitude and loneliness. No other characters were in the play and the setting was stark and colorless. There seemed to be no real purpose to what the lone performer was doing in the play. This was a startling realization for me, and I decided to make some changes to add relationships, fun, and social activity to my life. I was living with an expectation of ending up alone at the end of the "play."

To learn more about life scripts, read *Scripts People Live*, by Claude Steiner. See Additional Reading for more information.

Discovering Psychological Drivers

An award-winning psychologist, Taibi Kahler, discovered that everyone has powerful psychological forces that influence moment-to-moment thinking, feeling, and behaving. He called these forces drivers because we feel driven when these psychological forces kick in. We are driven to prove that we are okay—we don't want to feel not okay!

How do we get these drivers? All small children want to be loved and to have the approval of significant adults such as parents, grandparents, teachers, and others. As very young children we all tried to figure out what we had to do to make sure that we had the love and approval we craved.

Do you recall hearing lines such as the following:

"Be careful—stay in the lines when you are coloring!"

"Stop crying—you're not hurt that bad."

"Oh, thank you, sweetie! I just love you to pieces when you do nice things like that for me!"

"Get a move on! You're going to be late!"

"No, I won't help you do it. You just do it again until you get it right."

We all grow up hearing messages such as these. Young children not only hear and see everything going on around them, they record it all. It is as if we are all equipped with audiovideo recorders at birth and these messages become a library of tapes that stay with us forever!

Defining the Five Drivers

We all learn the same standards for proving that we are worthwhile and deserving of the love and acceptance that we crave. We also use these standards to help accomplish the life script we chose for ourselves. We all have all five drivers in our psychological program, but one or two will be primary. Different personality types have different dominant drivers. The five psychological drivers are defined as follows:

Be Perfect

This psychological driver tells us that to be okay we have to strive for perfection in all that we do. Plan, think before you speak, work carefully, double-check to make sure there are no mistakes, avoid things that cannot be done perfectly, organize, systematize, and make sure you have done everything possible to avoid errors. People who have this driver as their most powerful one tend to over-explain, over-detail, and talk in long, complex sentences to make sure they have communicated perfectly.

Please Others

This driver urges us to place others' needs above our own, to anticipate what makes others happy, to make special effort to do what others will like, and to make sure that we do nothing that will offend or hurt someone's feelings. We think that to be okay we must prove to others that we care about them and never act in a way that would be considered selfish. People with this dominant driver defer to others and place others' needs above their own to the extent that they often will not be honest about their own wants and needs.

Be Strong

This driver says that to be okay we must deny pain and keep going no matter how difficult the going becomes. We must tough it out, never ask for help, never admit that we do not know how or cannot do it alone, show others that we are capable of doing without any help, and never let them see fear, doubt, or sadness. Showing such emotions is perceived as weakness. People with this driver find it difficult to trust others and have problems with closeness and intimacy. They hide their feelings and maintain distance in their relationships because they have a difficult time trusting others and admitting that they need anyone or anything from others. They are uncomfortable with their own emotions.

Try Hard

This driver message results in valuing effort more than results. This driver leads us to try and try but often fail—because what is important is to keep trying. We struggle, get confused, take on more than we can handle, find difficulties and complications, and then have to keep trying harder and harder to keep up, finish on schedule, or just get done at all. People with a strong dose of this driver tend to take pride only in achievements that were really difficult, while discounting the value of things that come easily. They often fall short of their goals and have a lot of stress because everything in life is so difficult.

Hurry Up

This driver urges us to zip from one thing to another as we race through life with a constant feeling of being behind schedule. We feel anxious about not having enough time to get everything done so we go faster, but our haste results in mistakes, forgetting things, false starts, and the like, and we get even farther behind. When we are responding to this driver, we will over-schedule, sleep through the morning alarm, misplace important things such as car keys, and end up having to hurry. People with this driver as their primary one are notoriously late and disorganized.

Analyzing the Drivers' Negative Impact

Even though the psychological drivers served us when we were very young by giving us ways to feel okay about ourselves, they can be hindrances in adulthood. They are similar to training wheels that helped us learn to ride a bicycle—now that we know how to ride a bike, they keep getting in the way!

Think about how each of the drivers may be limiting your effectiveness or satisfaction in various aspects of your life. On the lines that follow each driver below, note how that driver has a negative impact on you.

Be Perfect _____

_____

_____

_____

Please Others _____

_____

_____

_____

Be Strong _____

_____

_____

_____

Try Hard _____

_____

_____

_____

Hurry Up _____

_____

_____

_____

The first step in diminishing the negative impact of the drivers on how you live your life is recognizing them so you know what you need to change. You can identify your drivers by becoming aware of what you say, what you do, and how you handle various situations. The exercises on the next few pages will help you do this.

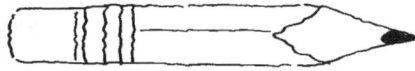

HEAR WHAT YOU SAY

Practice identifying the drivers in the following examples. Write the abbreviation for each one in the space provided.

BP = Be Perfect   BS = Be Strong   PO = Please Others
HU = Hurry Up   TH = Try Hard

_____ 1. "Oh, you decide. I'll be glad to see whatever you want to see."

_____ 2. "I'm okay. It's just a scratch."

_____ 3. "From here you drive north 6.7 miles, turn right at the intersection where the convenience store is located on the northeast corner, proceed in an easterly direction for 3.4 miles to Spruce Street, turn left and drive north two blocks and look for the white colonial house with a large maple tree in the front yard. The address is 1716 Spruce. Park on the left side of the driveway so John can pull his car into the garage when he gets home. He is due home from a meeting at 7:15, which will be about a half hour after you arrive."

_____ 4. "Oh, wow, I am really late! I gotta go. Catch you later."

_____ 5. "How does this thing work? I never can figure out what to do first with this crazy thing and the instruction manual just gets me more confused."

_____ 6. "Look, I told you I'm feeling fine. I just felt a little dizzy for a minute. No big deal."

_____ 7. "Are you sure it's okay for me to go to the game without you?"

_____ 8. "What exactly did you have in mind?"

_____ 9. "Well, I'm pretty busy on Thursday but I guess I could squeeze you in between a couple of appointments if I grab lunch at my desk. Come by at about 1:30."

_____ 10. "There was something I wanted to tell you and now I can't think what it was! My mind is a blank!"

Compare your answers with the authors' responses in the Appendix

SEEING YOUR DRIVERS IN YOUR BELIEFS AND VALUES

Our beliefs and values can also reveal our drivers. This exercise lists five alternatives for each of five beliefs or values. Read each statement and on the line before each one, identify the driver it exemplifies. Use the same abbreviations as in the preceding exercise.

The way to succeed in work is to:

____ 1. Be sure that every assignment is completed by using all my skills to the best of my ability.

____ 2. Receive any and all assignments without complaint—even when I dislike them or disagree with them.

____ 3. Accomplish an assignment in the shortest period of time possible.

____ 4. Try to get as much done as I can each day.

____ 5. Always do what I am asked and get along well with others.

In work and recreation it is best to:

____ 1. Always take pride in seeing a task through to completion with great accuracy.

____ 2. Really enjoy being around to do things for other people.

____ 3. Take on more responsibility even if it means having to put forth extra effort.

____ 4. Have many projects going on at once even though it might be difficult to complete them in a short time.

____ 5. Always do what I am asked and get along well with others.

A good approach to decision-making is:

____ 1. Look for answers that will make everybody happy.

____ 2. Make quick decisions to avoid procrastinating.

____ 3. Put a lot of effort into making the right decision.

____ 4. Examine completely every aspect of a problem before taking action to solve it.

____ 5. Take complete responsibility for all of the decisions in which I am involved.

CONTINUED

In living life, the following beliefs guide me:

____ 1. I believe that the way to succeed in life is to keep trying no matter how many times you fail.

____ 2. I believe that a person should never settle for less than the best when the best is available.

____ 3. I believe that a person does what has to be done and that you can rise to any occasion.

____ 4. I believe that if you take care of others, they will take care of you in return.

____ 5. I believe that a person should never put off until tomorrow what can be done today.

As a parent and/or a life partner, I should:

____ 1. Do everything I can to make others happy and not be selfish.

____ 2. Be an example and show others how to think clearly and live in an organized and efficient manner.

____ 3. Not burden others with my problems and take care of myself.

____ 4. Do as many things as I can possibly handle and not inconvenience anyone by taking too long.

____ 5. Devote all of my energies to the difficult task of making the family work and not be casual with my responsibilities.

Compare your answers with the authors' responses in the Appendix.

By now you may have already decided which of the drivers are most powerful for you. If you have not, go back through these last two exercises and place checkmarks (✔) beside each message that seems closest to the way you talk and the way you think. This may help you discover the one or two drivers that influence how you are living your life.

Observing How Drivers Affect Life Balance

From your reading thus far, you have seen how the psychological drivers can have a strong impact on your values and beliefs. And you have analyzed possible negative effects. This section looks at the ways that each driver tends to affect a person's life balance.

Be Perfect

Individuals for whom this driver is dominant tend to be "workaholics." Because "Be Perfect" urges people to be thorough, precise, and accurate, these individuals spend a lot time with each project, making sure it is done perfectly. They plan, schedule, and calculate their every move. This driver works against spontaneity and fun, so individuals with a large dose of "Be Perfect" tend to play only when they have scheduled playtime. Even then they often have a difficult time relaxing and enjoying themselves because they are thinking about what they must do when playtime is over.

Another result of the "Be Perfect" driver is the tendency to be overly critical of what others do and how they do it, which can interfere with the quality of relationships. It is not enjoyable for others to be corrected frequently or to be told of their lack of accuracy or timeliness. Such annoying patterns can make it difficult to meet life balance goals related to relationships (friends, family) and social activities.

Did this explanation prompt another idea or two about how this driver affects you and your life? If so, jot those thoughts here:

_____

_____

_____

_____

Please Others

Individuals for whom this driver is dominant can have a difficult time achieving the life balance they desire because they are constantly putting other people's needs before their own. They have a longtime pattern of putting personal preferences, wants, and needs farther down the list after first taking care of others. Many who have "Please Others" as their dominant driver do not know what they want and need because they have a habit of not focusing on themselves and do not have "permission" to allow their own wants and needs to even be considered. These individuals often start feeling dissatisfied and may even feel used by others— unaware that they have done it to themselves.

Individuals with a strong "Please Others" driver also tend to believe that everyone should be aware of others' needs and make extra effort to do nice things for others. They often see self-directed people as selfish or insensitive, and this can cause a strain in relationships. Others can become frustrated with "Please Others" individuals who will not express their own preferences in deference to others. Some people will take advantage of "Please Others" individuals who always let others have their way.

Did this explanation prompt another idea or two about how this driver affects you and your life? If so, jot those thoughts here:

_____

_____

_____

_____

Be Strong

Individuals for whom this driver is dominant do not allow others to get close. The "Be Strong" driver pushes individuals to be self-contained and reluctant to share with others because they believe this would be weak. Instead, they themselves must bear all the troubles, fears, hurts, and the like without complaint and without burdening others because, after all, "when the going gets tough, the tough get going!" This may affect life balance because these individuals take on too many responsibilities. And they will not ask for help, which they see as a sign of weakness or inadequacy.

Relationships for "Be Strong" individuals remain at arm's length with little genuine intimacy. Others feel shut out by people with high "Be Strong" drivers. "Be Strong" individuals can develop serious health problems because they are not in tune with their own body, they ignore symptoms or they expect them to go away, and they do not seek medical help. They are very likely to succumb to problems caused by stress because they refuse to acknowledge the stress.

Did this explanation prompt another idea or two about how this driver affects you and your life? If so, jot those thoughts here:

_____

_____

_____

_____

Try Hard

Individuals for whom this driver is dominant go through life experiencing many failures—big and small. The "Try Hard" driver causes a pattern of expending much effort with little to show for it. Such individuals will subconsciously commit to more than can be accomplished and then feel pressured to work hard, sweat, and strain in a vain effort to get it all done. These individuals have a difficult time achieving a balanced life because they do not accomplish many goals. They have difficulty focusing on what is important to them because they have so much going on. They try and try, but do not often succeed.

Even more frustrating for "Try Hard" individuals is that they feel little satisfaction from the accomplishments that do come easily. The only achievements they value are those that require extreme effort. This driver also can cause individuals to disapprove of others who do not seem to work as hard as they do even if the others do get things accomplished. Someone for whom this driver is dominant will reward those who simply work hard, even if they do not get as much done as people who are better organized and achieve more—but seem not to work hard.

Did this explanation prompt another idea or two about how this driver affects you and your life? If so, jot those thoughts here:

_____

_____

_____

_____

Hurry Up

Individuals for whom this driver is dominant race through life in a mad dash but always seem to be behind schedule. They have a pattern of finishing assignments late, showing up for appointments or social events late, procrastinating and doing things (such as tax returns) at the last minute, and feeling anxious a great deal of the time. This driver tends to prevent achieving a life balance that includes time for relaxation, extended time with friends or family, long conversations, and so on because of the constant pressure to hurry on to the next thing.

"Hurry Up" individuals also prompt discomfort in others with their signals for others to hurry. They will tap a pencil on the conference table like a drummer, look at their watch repeatedly, fidget, motion for others to speed up by using a wind-up gesture, and talk rapidly, which results in others feeling pressured. Others often want to escape from "Hurry Up" behaviors.

Did this explanation prompt another idea or two about how this driver affects you and your life? If so, jot those thoughts here:

_____

_____

_____

_____

Remember, everyone has these psychological drivers. We just do not have them in equal amounts. Your primary drivers are the ones that will have the most impact on your behaviors and your life balance.

Reprogramming Your Drivers

As you have learned, your own psychological drivers can cause you to feel bad about yourself because you are not living up to the drivers' unrealistic standards. But what if it were possible to reduce your drivers' impact on your life patterns and life balance? This goal is achievable.

At first, people may be reluctant to change their drivers because they think that many of the messages are positive and have helped them often during their lives. And they are right. Remember, these drivers began as coping mechanisms that helped us survive and feel okay.

Indeed, you need not abandon the underlying values and beliefs on which the drivers are based to improve the quality of your life, work, and relationships. All you need to do is to redefine the expectations to make them more flexible and realistic. This will allow you to feel less stressed and to achieve your goals more easily.

Step by Step

Psychological reprogramming is a fairly simple process, but it does take time and commitment. In this age of quick fixes and instant gratification, we have come to expect fast results! Reprogramming a computer requires only deleting old software and installing new. But reprogramming ourselves is a much slower process that requires installing the new program many times before it will operate.

You can redefine your expectations by following this three-step process:

Step 1: Examine each of your drivers and the subconscious messages and belief systems that support each one to discover how it is unrealistic and how it contributes to problems.

Step 2: Set new standards or expectations that will retain the underlying values and allow you to be what you want to be with less strain and fewer obstacles.

Step 3: Program these more realistic standards into your subconscious so they guide you rather than the driver messages previously there.

The next sections will guide you through this process in detail.

Rethinking Your Underlying Messages

There is nothing wrong with living your life according to any of the five psychological drivers. For the most part, the driver messages are positive. But problems can arise from trying to adhere to the driver(s) too rigidly and thus setting yourself up for failure. What will help you is to be more flexible in your thinking as you follow the guidelines of the drivers.

With each of the following messages, identify what is unrealistic about it and, on the line provided, write a more realistic, achievable message to replace it.

"Be Perfect" Messages

Strive for perfection _____

Expect others to be perfect _____

Be precisely accurate _____

Follow every rule _____

Cover all the bases _____

Be understood exactly _____

"Be Strong" Messages

Hold in and hide feelings _____

Don't care or get involved _____

Stay one up on others _____

Always be calm and in control _____

Keep others at a distance; don't touch _____

Be tough—not soft and weak _____

"Please Others" Messages

Be approved of by others _____

Always be nice _____

Do for others first_____

You should show you care and offer help _____

Always be agreeable and cooperative _____

Defer to others; do not argue _____

"Try Hard" Messages

Try harder_____

Find difficulties and obstacles _____

Start more than you can finish _____

Push to get it done _____

Be proud only when you do something difficult _____

Success is 10% inspiration, 90% perspiration _____

"Hurry Up" Messages

Do things faster—get a move on _____

Do everything right now _____

Hurry others along _____

Never relax (got to keep going!) _____

Interrupt others_____

Just speed up and you'll catch up _____

Did you find it difficult to define more realistic and achievable standards? It is likely that the ones most difficult for you were your own most powerful driver messages. These are the most important ones for you to alter.

The more realistic messages you adopt to counteract your driver messages are called "allower" messages. Examples are in the Appendix. These may help you compare and possibly improve the messages you created yourself. Getting new messages into your subconscious will allow you to reduce stress, achieve more goals, and get your life balance where you want it.

Installing Your "Allower" Messages

When you have established more realistic messages, the next step is to install these allower messages into your subconscious mind. The reason that driver messages have such a powerful effect on us and how we live our lives is that they are buried in our subconscious and drive us to prove over and over that we are okay. The allower messages also must be imbedded in our subconscious to offset the drivers and allow us to think, act, and feel differently.

Relaxation and Installation

Choose a time when you will go through the reprogramming process each day. Pick a time when you will be willing to spend 15 minutes or more daily. Some people prefer early morning while others prefer just before bedtime. Many find that the bedtime choice has an additional benefit of helping you sleep more soundly and restfully.

At this time each day first achieve deep relaxation. Use one or several of the following techniques to help you relax completely:

> Exercise vigorously

> Take a hot bath (add bubbles!) or shower

> Lower the lights

> Light a scented candle

> Listen to soft, relaxing music (baroque music can be effective)

> Starting with your toes, tighten your muscles, hold the tension five or six seconds, release the tension, tense them again and add another muscle group, hold and release, and continue the process until you reach the tips of your fingers and the top of your head

When you are fully relaxed, take no more than five of your new allower messages and read them aloud to yourself. Read each message several times before moving to the next one. Read the message with conviction. Believe it. Listen to your voice, hear the message, visualize yourself following the message, feel the emotions associated with the message.

Do this with each message. The more you can believe the truth of the message and see yourself living the message, the more powerfully it will become fixed in your subconscious mind.

Repeat the relaxation and installation steps daily for at least 21 days. Remember, this is not a quick fix! If you do this daily, you will discover that you start thinking, feeling, and acting differently because your subconscious messages will affect your perceptions of daily events and situations. This will prompt you to make different decisions than you would have with the previous driver messages.

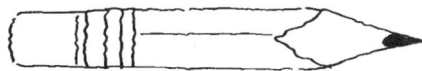

CHANGING YOUR INTERNAL DIALOGUE

Now that you know about psychological drivers and how they affect your daily life and your life balance, you can reduce the impact of the messages by monitoring your thoughts and word choices.

Listen to your internal dialogue and notice the language. When you hear driver language, change it to allower language.

Hear what you say when interacting with others and notice the driver language. Practice using new language that is more "allowing" and realistic in your expectations of self and others. Use the examples that follow to practice. Rewrite each one into a message that is free of driver language.

Maybe we could find a less expensive place to stay if that would be okay with you? ("Please Others" driver)

_____

_____

_____

Oh, man! I'll never be able to do this right! ("Try Hard")

_____

_____

_____

No, dear. Their house is not three blocks from that intersection; it is four blocks, the third house on the right, which is .36 miles from the intersection. ("Be Perfect")

_____

_____

_____

CONTINUED

================================ CONTINUED ================================

Gosh! Look at the time! We better get a move on or we'll never make it on time. ("Hurry Up")

_____

_____

_____

The layoffs have forced us all to put in long hours. You should be glad you still have a job. ("Be Strong")

_____

_____

_____

Compare your rewritten versions with the authors' responses
in the Appendix.

Remember that you will always have the drivers as part of your personality. But when you learn to be more aware of them and reduce their impact on your behavior, language, feelings, and choices, you will be more empowered to live your life according to your chosen values and priorities. Rather than allowing unrealistic expectations to drive you in directions that might not be the best for you and others, you can make more conscious choices that will give you and others greater satisfaction.

Managing Your

Time

Setting Priorities According to Your Values

Most of us have moments when we feel overwhelmed by all of our duties and the many demands on our time. An important part of achieving a balanced life is learning to manage how you use your time.

After identifying your values and priorities, the next step is to translate them into goals. Effective time management is using your time to accomplish high-priority goals that help you satisfy your values, rather than spending time on things that do not help you achieve what is truly important to you.

Remember, a goal is not a plan. It is not an activity. It is not what you do. A goal is a *statement of something you plan to achieve*. It is a target, a result that you want.

Each of your goals is not equally important, so you must assign priorities to them. An easy way to do this is to use an A-B-C system in line with your A, B, and C values. A goal related to an A value is assigned an A.

This is important because when you are busy living your life and working toward achieving your goals, you often have to make decisions about how to use your time. The basic rule is to *use your time to do something toward achieving an A priority goal.*

Many people spend a lot of their time doing things that are related to C goals. Why do you think this is?

_____

_____

_____

For many people, C goals are easier and faster to achieve, and people like to get quick results. This way they also feel they are getting more accomplished. Achieving an A goal can take weeks, months, even years.

But when you stop to think about it, the same amount of time devoted to getting something accomplished related to an A goal is by definition more important for you than knocking off a C. Your own evaluation told you that the A was most important and most valued.

Making Effective Use of To-Do Lists

An important part of managing your time is your action plan, listing all of your action steps toward accomplishing your goal. This action plan will be most effective if you also include timelines for completing the action steps. The timelines will be helpful to you as you write a daily to-do list.

Do you use a daily to-do list? Does it work well for you or do you find that you still do not get as much done as you intended?

Common problems with to-do lists include writing tasks on multiple pieces of paper (Post-it notes, backs of envelopes, napkins), using the same list day after day, and failing to assign priorities to the items on the list. Guilty of any of these?

> ➤ Make a new list each day. It is okay to carry over some items from the day before but create a new list because the priorities can change.

> ➤ Assign A, B, and C priorities to the tasks on the list. This is relatively easy when you have written goals with A, B, and C priorities assigned. The action steps that lead to the accomplishment of an A goal are assigned an A priority on the daily to-accomplish list.

> ➤ Do the A tasks, not the Cs. Most people do Cs because they are easier and faster, so they give you the satisfaction of crossing items off the list. You feel productive. But the point of priorities is to help you use your time to accomplish important things, so let the Cs be carried over day after day, if necessary, until the important things have been done.

Overwhelming A-Priority Tasks

You may be thinking that some A-priority tasks take more than a day to complete while other things on your list also need to be done. Alan Lakein, a noted time management expert, refers to such an A task as an "overwhelming A." A long, involved task can be dangerous because you will be tempted to keep putting it off until you have time to do it. That may result in your never doing it. Have you ever said, "I just never got around to it?" Of course you have.

Lakein recommends using the "Swiss cheese technique" on an overwhelming A. What he means is to poke holes in it (like Swiss cheese) until finally it is all done. Break down the task into smaller steps and do them until the whole task has been done. When you stop to think about it, 20 or 30 minutes devoted to achieving a little bit of an A task is a better use of your time than knocking off two or three C priority tasks. Remember that, by definition, an A is more important than a C.

Handling Paperwork and E-Mail Efficiently

Another time management challenge is how to handle all of the paperwork and e-mail that comes in every day. How much time do you spend each day on paper and e-mail?

Assigning Priorities

The A-B-C system can help you deal with paperwork and e-mail more efficiently. When you receive new paper and new e-mail messages, assign each item a priority. With paper, you can place each document in one of three stacks or folders. With e-mail messages, you can move each message into one of three folders. The next step is to reevaluate each document in the B stack or folder and decide if it needs action today. If the answer is yes, move it to the A stack/folder. If the answer is no, move it to the C stack/folder.

The next step is important and sometimes difficult. Look at each item in the A stack/folder and take whatever action is needed. Do it now and get it out of the way. Handle each document only once. It is tempting to keep returning to important items but you have a list waiting for your attention, so you need to do what needs to be done and not return to that same document. This requires discipline but it can make a dramatic difference in how much you get done in the time you have available.

Keeping Low-Priority Items in Their Place

What about the C stack? A useful technique is to designate a drawer in your desk as the C drawer and to drop the C documents into that drawer each day and close the drawer so you will not be tempted to even look at those items again. Do the same with the C folder in your e-mail program. Do not open the folder until after you have acted on the A items and accomplished the A tasks on your daily to-accomplish list. The time you spend with C papers and e-mail messages is time that could be used to accomplish something more important.

Using this approach with the paperwork that comes in each day often results in much of the daily paper going into the C drawer. When the drawer is filled to capacity, it can be moved to a cardboard box. Then if you need a document that was placed in the C drawer, you can find it and act on it. But most of the paper that goes into the C drawer never comes out again—until it goes into the recycle bin!

You will find that the same will be true of your C folder in the e-mail program. Eventually, you will delete most of the messages that went into the C folder. Many people generate paper and e-mail messages that do not relate to your A and B priorities. Do not allow them to control how you use your time! You will be more productive when you take the few minutes to assess the documents and act only on the important ones.

Keeping a Time Log

A time log can help you see how you are using your time. This can help you identify opportunities to use your time more productively.

How do you do this? Use a blank sheet of paper or create a chart on which you will enter what you did during each 30-minute time period during the day, as in the following example:

8:00-8:30	Read mail, sorted, responded to A stuff
8:30-9:00	Returned important phone calls, searched for info. on Internet for first A task
9:00-9:30	Met with boss
9:30-10:00	Brainstorming meeting with team for solutions to urgent problem
10:00-11:00	10 min. break, worked on PowerPoint presentation on another A task
11:00-12:00	More work on PP presentation, returned calls that came in during morning
12:00-1:00	Lunch with spouse and meeting with travel agent about vacation plans

When you keep a time log for a few weeks, you will be able to determine what things are taking the largest amounts of your time and energy. You may be able to see if you need to change how you are using your time to allow you to devote more time to more important goals and tasks.

Beware Time Robbers

You may also notice that certain people are taking a lot of your time, and that time may be very nonproductive. Indeed, many people discover that the biggest time robbers are other people. It is easy to allow others to steal your time when you are not being attentive and when you are not assertive with others.

If you allow them, some people will take a lot of your time and energy to meet their own needs. This means that you are working to achieve their goals rather than your own (unless one of your high-priority values is helping others). When you give away your time and energy, you are likely to find that your life is out of balance.

The exercise on the following page will help you determine how good you are at devoting time and energy to your own values and goals rather than to those of others.

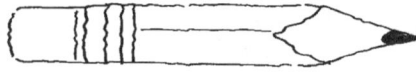

ARE OTHER PEOPLE "STEALING" YOUR TIME?

Read the statement in the right-hand column, and then check (✔) the box in the left-hand column that indicates how often the statement is true for you.

Always	Usually	Half the Time	Seldom	Never	
❑	❑	❑	❑	❑	I say no when someone asks me to do something I do not want to do.
❑	❑	❑	❑	❑	I feel good about how much I accomplish each day.
❑	❑	❑	❑	❑	My friends/family know they can count on me to help when needed.
❑	❑	❑	❑	❑	I enjoy doing things with my friends.
❑	❑	❑	❑	❑	I appreciate being asked to do things for others.
❑	❑	❑	❑	❑	I regret using my leisure time on others' projects and activities.
❑	❑	❑	❑	❑	I resent having to work overtime.
❑	❑	❑	❑	❑	I wish I had more time for my own wants and needs.

There are no "right answers" for this quiz and only you can evaluate the results. Ask yourself how you feel about each response. The best indicator is your own emotional response. For example, if you feel anxious or annoyed about how you answered the first question, that is a clue that you need to improve how you respond to requests for help.

When you agree to do things you do not want to do, you are not taking care of your own wants and needs. If you do not feel good about how much you accomplish or about what you are doing for or with others, then that is a sign that you can improve how you use your time in relation to your own priorities.

Managing Your Relationships

Evaluating Your Relationships

Success in managing your relationships means that the time you give to others gives you rewards that are important to you. This part will help you manage your relationships better so you will be more satisfied with how you use your time and what you achieve.

Thinking about the time you spend on each of your relationships may give you insight into whether the relationship adds satisfaction to your life or subtracts, whether it supports or detracts from a balanced life. The following two-step process will help you make this analysis.

Step 1: In the left-hand column below, write the names or initials of individuals in your life—family, friends, co-workers, customers/clients, supervisors/managers, neighbors, members of social or professional groups, and so on.

Person	Adds to my Life Balance	Subtracts from my Life Balance

Step 2: Think about your relationship with each individual and indicate in the other two columns how the person adds to or subtracts from your life balance. You may find that some people do both. For example, one person may be a source of emotional support when you need it, which adds to your life balance. But that same person may also expect you to spend a lot of time with him when you would prefer to use your time differently. This would interfere with your life balance.

After completing the exercise, you may find that some of your relationships are subtracting more from your life balance than they are adding. Then you will benefit from making changes in those relationships.

If some of your relationships are neutral, you may want to reduce the time and energy you devote to those relationships. Then you would be able to use more of your time and energy in relationships that are positive, which would help you achieve the life balance you desire.

Understanding the Skill of Assertiveness

The conversations you have with others to improve or maintain your life balance are some of the most important interactions you will ever have. An important skill for these communications is assertiveness. Let's take a look at how assertive behavior differs from nonassertive behavior or aggressive behavior.

Nonassertive Behavior

Nonassertive individuals do not stand up effectively for their rights or express their thoughts, feelings, opinions, wants, or needs. They speak up only in a passive, indirect, and ineffective manner. Nonassertive behavior communicates uncertainty or a lack of confidence or power. The message that others detect: *I am not as good as you; I don't count; my wants and needs are not as important as yours; you don't have to pay attention to me.* Nonassertive individuals allow others to win at their expense. Behaving nonassertively often results in feeling like a "victim". Sometimes being nonassertive results in playing "rescuer" – doing for others when you really don't want to!

Aggressive Behavior

Aggressive individuals speak up, but they do so in a manner that others find inappropriate and disrespectful. While standing up for their own rights, they violate the rights of others. Aggressive behavior can be hostile and threatening, or sarcastic, or condescending, or even charming and friendly while being dishonest and manipulative. The message to others: *I am better than you; you don't count; your ideas, wants and needs don't matter.* The goal is to win and make sure that others lose. Aggressive behavior results in being perceived as a "persecutor" by others who see themselves as your "victims". A more subtle way of demonstrating superiority is to "rescue" others by doing things for them that they are quite capable of doing for themselves. This also invites them to feel like a "victim".

Assertive Behavior

Assertive individuals speak up in a manner that comes across as direct, honest, appropriate, and respectful. Assertive behavior communicates confidence and self-awareness along with an awareness of and respect for others. The message: *We both are okay; we are equals; our wants, needs, rights, values, and goals are equally important.* Assertive behavior has a win-win objective.

Everyone uses all three of these behavior styles from time to time. The exercise on the following page will help you identify which behavior style you use most often.

WHICH BEHAVIOR STYLE ARE YOU?

Complete the quiz below to get an idea of which behavior style comes most naturally to you. Check (✓) the box that best reflects you.

V = Very much like you   S = Somewhat like you   N = Not at all like you

V	S	N	
❑	❑	❑	1. When others ask what I think, I give them my honest opinion even if it is different from theirs.
❑	❑	❑	2. If I am served food that is not prepared the way I expected, I send it back.
❑	❑	❑	3. I ask directly for what I want or tell others my preferences.
❑	❑	❑	4. When speaking with higher-ranking people, I feel confident and think clearly.
❑	❑	❑	5. I comfortably say no when someone asks me to do something I do not want or like to do.
❑	❑	❑	6. In groups I will offer ideas about how to proceed.
❑	❑	❑	7. When playing sports or other games, I like to win but can enjoy playing even when I lose.
❑	❑	❑	8. When I disagree with someone, it is usually because I know my opinion is right.
❑	❑	❑	9. I am comfortable delegating or asking someone to do something, and I trust that they will do it well.
❑	❑	❑	10. In social situations I will initiate contact with strangers.

CONTINUED

If you checked mostly V, you may be either consistently assertive or aggressive. You are likely to have high self-esteem. Which of the two styles you actually use depends on how you communicate in those situations. Both assertive and aggressive behavior can be direct and active, but aggressive behavior differs in that you are perceived as pushy, abrasive, disrespectful, or inconsiderate because of the words and body language you use. When you are assertive, you are perceived as appropriate and respectful.

If you checked mostly S, you probably are fairly assertive and at times will choose to be nonassertive rather than take the risk of appearing pushy or offending someone.

If you checked mostly N, you are more nonassertive and find it challenging to feel comfortable standing up for yourself.

Increasing Your Assertiveness

If you tend to be more aggressive or nonassertive, you can become more effective in managing your relationships if you increase the frequency of your assertiveness and decrease how much you use the other two behavior styles.

Why become more assertive? As the table below outlines, nonassertive individuals accomplish few of their goals because they tend to defer to others rather than focus on their own needs. Aggressive individuals may accomplish most of their goals, but at a high cost to their relationships. Study the table to compare and contrast the tendencies in each behavior type.

	Nonassertive	Assertive	Aggressive
Goals accomplished	Few; defer to others	Most; willing to compromise	Most; I win, you lose—no compromise
Reputation	Pushover, easy to beat	Cooperative, fair, confident	Ruthless, abrasive
Relationships	Depend on doing for others, putting others first	Based on mutual trust and cooperation	Competitive; little trust results in minimal sharing
Handling conflict	Plays victim—others "rescue" or "persecute"—defer to avoid conflict	Differences are resolved with open communication; minimal conflict	Plays "persecutor" or "rescuer" to prove superiority; creates conflict
Time usage	Won't say no; allows others to determine use of time	Decides how to use time based on goals/priorities; says no appropriately	Uses others' time; doesn't consider others' values and priorities

How can you increase your assertiveness? If you tend to be nonassertive, you will benefit from learning how to build your self-esteem. You can do this with the aid of self-help books and training programs. You also can become aware of how you communicate with others and practice using assertive words and delivery. With practice, it does get easier.

If you tend to be aggressive, you will benefit from developing your empathy—the ability to be aware of what others need and how they feel. Improving your listening skills can help you develop this ability. Also pay attention to how you communicate with others and practice using assertive words and delivery.

If you are more assertive, then others will be more likely to hear your wants and needs and cooperate with you to achieve a better life balance. Again, with practice, it does get easier.

Read *Developing Positive Assertiveness* by Sam R. Lloyd, Thomson Learning/Course Technology.

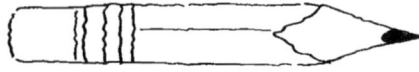

RECOGNIZING BEHAVIOR STYLES

An accurate awareness of all three behavior styles will help you be more consistently assertive. Evaluate the following examples to test your ability to recognize each style. Indicate in the space before each statement whether the statement shows nonassertive (N), assertive (AS), or aggressive (AG) behavior.

_____ 1. "I guess that would be okay. I mean, if that's what you really want to do, then I think I might enjoy it."

_____ 2. "Grab your coat, honey! We're going to the movies with the Meekers."

_____ 3. "That has to be the worst suggestion I've ever heard."

_____ 4. "I need some help with this section, Madison. Will you give me some suggestions, please?"

_____ 5. "Oh well, I'm very busy but if it's really important, I might be able to spare a few minutes."

_____ 6. "Why do you always expect me to take the kids to their activities? You're their parent, too, you know!"

_____ 7. "I'm frustrated because I seem to be the one who is responsible for transporting the kids to their activities and I want us to work out a way to share that responsibility."

_____ 8. "Do you think we could handle some of the household stuff differently?"

_____ 9. "You know, it would be nice if I could take a couple of my vacation days next week so I could spend some time with my old friend who is visiting from Europe—if it wouldn't be too inconvenient."

_____ 10. "I just learned that an old friend will be in town next week for a few days and I would like to spend some time with her while she is here. May I take a couple of my vacation days next Thursday and Friday?"

Compare your answers with the authors' responses in the Appendix.

Communicating Assertively

Being aware of the different behavior styles is only the starting point. Learning to communicate with others assertively also requires choosing the right words and delivering them effectively. The following tips will help you practice doing that.

➤ Reduce or eliminate tentative, hesitant words and behaviors such as "maybe," "kind of," "only," "just," "I guess," "uh," "ah," pauses and shrugs.

➤ Reduce or eliminate exaggerations, negative judgments, accusations, pointing fingers, harsh voice tones, and disapproving facial expressions.

➤ Express your thoughts, feelings, opinions, wants, and needs with I statements, such as "I am concerned," "I prefer the other solution," or "I want to stay home tonight."

➤ Use polite commands or requests to get others to do things for you. "Please arrange a meeting with Fred and Sue." "Will you please review this report and prepare a summary for me?"

Practice Speaking Assertively

Imagine yourself in each of the following scenarios and write a response that would be communicating assertively.

➤ You hope your spouse or significant other will commit to planning your vacation trip because you do not enjoy doing that kind of thing and you need to catch up with your work so you can relax and enjoy the vacation.

What do you say to get this commitment? _____

_____

_____

➤ After evaluating your manager's offer of a new work assignment that would require moving to another city, you have decided to decline the offer because it does not align with your values and priorities. Even though the new assignment would increase your income, it would interfere with other plans and needs.

What will you say to communicate your decision to your manager? _____

_____

_____

Compare your answers with the authors' responses in the Appendix.

Balancing Relationships Through Contracts

Relationships can be a source of satisfaction and they can be a major complication. For many people, taking a contractual approach to relationships can reduce the problems and improve the odds that the relationship will be positive and rewarding. This is true with personal relationships and with those at work.

The idea is to make sure that each person has the same understanding of how the relationship will work and what each person's roles and commitments are. When these are openly negotiated and agreed on, and when each person has made a sincere commitment, many problems are prevented, and maintaining a balanced life becomes easier.

Contract Requirements

Several criteria for successful contracts will help you develop workable agreements with others. Each of these is important for making sure that all concerned are committed to the contract and that the agreement produces the desired results.

> ➢ **Mutual Agreement** – Each person must willingly agree to the contract. If someone has been coerced or has agreed because he is nonassertive, usually the outcome will be a broken agreement. That person will not keep his promise.

> ➢ **Mutual Benefit** – All parties gain something of value by keeping their commitment. If the contract does not provide equal benefit for all, it will be perceived as unfair and probably will not work. In a court of law, a unilateral contract will not be enforced.

> ➢ **Mutual Ability** – All parties must be able to do what they have promised. If someone makes an unrealistic commitment, the result will be a failure to perform and the contract will be broken.

> ➢ **Legal** – The contract must conform to the laws, policies, and rules in the situation. If an agreement is in conflict with a law or rule, the parties will be reluctant to carry it out and when someone refuses to keep the commitment, there will be no way to enforce the agreement.

The case study that follows is an example of a successful contract in action. As you read through it, circle or note in the text where the contract requirements are being met.

CASE STUDY: Adam Goes to College

Adam graduated from high school and moved to another city to live with his father and attend college. Adam's father, Robert, told him that he was welcome and that he and Adam's mother (Robert's former wife) had agreed to pay for tuition and books and provide Adam with an allowance so he could be a full-time student.

During Adam's first semester he had difficulty with a course and dropped it. The same thing happened in the second semester. Adam also telephoned his mother several times during those months to request more money because he was running short. She sent him money each time.

The parents became concerned that their son was not pursuing his education seriously and was not managing his money well. They decided to clarify the arrangement with Adam. During a three-way telephone conversation, they expressed their concerns and suggested that the three of them work out a more clearly defined understanding. Adam agreed that this would be a good idea.

The result was a written contract in which the parents stipulated how much money each would provide for Adam monthly, that his father would provide food and lodging, that Adam would complete 15 credit hours of courses each semester and maintain a B average. Adam was not allowed to ask for additional funds except in the form of a loan to be repaid with interest. The parents were not allowed to give Adam extra money except for gifts on special occasions such as birthdays or Christmas. All of these terms were negotiated in an open conversation and agreed on. No terms were dictated.

Adam completed the balance of his undergraduate degree without dropping another course and without asking for more money or borrowing. His grade point average on graduation was better than a B.

CONTINUED

Now answer the following questions and compare your answers with the authors' responses in the Appendix.

1. What do you think explains the difference in Adam's behavior and productivity?

   _____

2. Indicate if the contract between Adam and his parents met each of the contract requirements:

   a. Did each person willingly agree to the contract? ❑ Yes ❑ No

   b. Did all parties have something to gain by keeping their commitments? If so, what?

   _____

   _____

   c. Should all parties have been able to do what they promised? Were the commitments realistic? ❑ Yes ❑ No

   d. Was the contract legal? ❑ Yes ❑ No

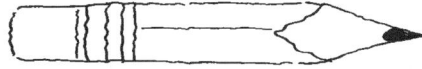

WHAT IS A VALID CONTRACT?

Evaluate each of the following contracts to determine if they fit the four contract requirements. If the contract fails to meet one or more of the criteria, write on the line provided which requirement(s) has been violated.

A parent tells a young child that he is now responsible for taking the trash to the curb each Tuesday by 7:30 A.M. for pickup and that the child's weekly allowance will be increased by $2. The child responds, "That means I'll have to get up even earlier, and the trash can is too heavy!" The parent replies, "You will only have to get up 10 minutes earlier and it is just one day a week and you are big enough to handle it. Now I need for you to do this. We all have to do our share in this family!"

Valid contract? ❑ Yes ❑ No

_____

A wife asks her husband to help her with household chores. He asks her what she wants him to do. She lists several things that she has always done (vacuuming carpets, washing and drying sheets and towels, and taking their daughter to dance classes). He rolls his eyes and says, "I'll be glad to take Becky to her dance classes but you know I hate housecleaning stuff!" She responds, "I really need some help now that I am working full-time and I want you to get something in return. I was thinking that you might enjoy having me take the kids somewhere a couple of evenings each month so you and your buddies could have your card games here at the house and you wouldn't have to worry about being raucous and watching your language with the kids around. Does that sound like a fair trade?" He answers, "Yeah! That's a great idea. You've got a deal!"

Valid contract? ❑ Yes ❑ No

_____

Compare your answers to the authors' responses in the Appendix.

CONTRACT WORKSHEET

Contracts work best when they meet all of the criteria and they are written. This worksheet will help you negotiate good contracts with others. There also is a sample of a written contract on the next page to help you compose your own.

1. What do I want? (Be specific)

    _____

    _____

2. What does the other party want? (Ask the other party and do not accept an answer of "nothing.")

    _____

    _____

3. Will you give what the other party wants? _____

4. Will the other party give what you want? _____

5. When will the contract begin? _____

6. When will the contract end? _____

7. Have you confirmed that each party is able to do what has been promised?

    _____

8. Does the contract violate any laws, rules, or existing contracts?

    _____

Sample Contract

I, Barbara, will give at least two hugs each day to Jason. In return I will receive from Jason the gift of his putting away his clothes after undressing each day. This contract will start on January 1, 20__ and will end on June 30, 20__.

If I become uncomfortable with this contract during that period, I will ask that it be renegotiated or terminated. At the ending date of the contract, I agree to negotiate with Jason about a renewal or changes in terms.

Signature and date

Maintaining Assertiveness While Negotiating

Even though the concept of contracting with others seems straightforward, the *process* of doing so can be challenging. It is important to be assertive when working out agreements for changes to improve your life balance. And even if *you* are assertive, others may become emotional and defensive when you negotiate with them because they are not accustomed to dealing with you in this manner. What do you do then?

For practice, consider how you would respond in the following negotiations. Write what you most likely would say or what you might do in each situation.

1. While negotiating with your spouse, he or she becomes agitated and says, "Why are you doing this? Are you telling me that our relationship is suddenly not good enough? This is insulting!"

_____

_____

_____

2. As you try to get your boss to agree to flextime to allow you to take college courses as a part-time student, she says, "I admire your ambition but I really can't agree to this kind of arrangement for you. We are shorthanded because of the cutbacks and I don't want to set a precedent for special deals."

_____

_____

_____

3. While you talk with your child about a contract for doing some household chores in exchange for an allowance increase, he says in a whining tone, "None of my friends have to work for their allowances and they all have more money to spend than I do! Why are you so mean?"

_____

_____

_____

Did you feel at a loss about what to say or do in these situations? Many people do not speak up because they do not know what to say or are afraid to say something. When they do speak up, they often fail to handle such incidents effectively.

Developing your assertiveness and listening skills will help you improve your relationships and do a better job when negotiating contracts with others. Both skills are powerful tools for improving or maintaining a balanced life.

The next sections focus on listening responses. From what you are about to learn, you will be able to evaluate your responses to the scenarios on the preceding page and perhaps see ways to improve your negotiations.

Responding to Others

Most of us receive no training in communication skills during our formative years when we are forming our communication habits. What little most people know about responding to life situations was learned from early life experiences and not from actual instruction. What most people learn to do is much the same as what others learn all over the world.

Nine Common Responses

The following are some of the most commonly used listening responses with brief explanations for each. As you read each one, think about whether you used that response in the preceding three situations.

1. Telling, Commanding

With this response, you tell the other person what to do (now or in the future). For example:

> ➤ "Stop that whining."

> ➤ "Calm down and I will explain."

> ➤ "Just listen for a few minutes and you will understand."

2. Moralizing, Preaching, Expressing Shoulds and Oughts

With these responses, you tell the other person what is best for them or for the situation by pushing your own beliefs or standards. For example:

> ➤ "All relationships have room for improvement and we should give this a try."

> ➤ "Children need to learn that privileges always come with responsibilities."

3. Advising, Offering Suggestions

Less pushy than preaching, this response attempts to help the other person by giving advice or possible solutions for a situation or problem. For example:

> ➤ "You can probably complete most of your courses with an e-learning program that wouldn't require going to classes."

> ➤ "If you would put half of your new allowance into a savings account, you would be able to buy some really nice things like your friends have."

4. Complimenting, Praising, or Agreeing

You attempt to get on the other person's good side by flattering or taking his or her side. For example:

➤ "You are a really smart person and you can figure out why some of your friends have more money than you."

➤ "You are right. We have a very good relationship."

5. Explaining, Being Logical

A common response to someone else's becoming emotional is to counter with logic and explanations in an attempt to get them to calm down and listen to reason. For example:

➤ "I am only attempting to improve our relationship by using an approach that I read about in a book about life balance."

➤ "An article in *Business Week* said that the most profitable organizations are using flextime arrangements with employees and experiencing improved productivity, improved loyalty, and reduced turnover."

6. Reassuring, Encouraging, Offering Sympathy

Another common response when others become emotional is to offer support by saying something you hope will help them feel better. For example:

➤ "Honey, you will feel much happier with our relationship when we work out a better way to share responsibilities and manage things so we can have more quality time together."

➤ "Sweetie, your mom and I want you to have nice things and grow up to be a happy person and we will do all we can to help you."

7. Asking Questions

Many people respond to what others say by asking fact-finding questions or questions that can be answered with either yes or no or a one-word reply. For example:

➤ "If I can get one of the others to agree to work the other hours, would you agree to this arrangement?"

➤ "Do you think our relationship has no room for improvement?"

➤ "Do any of your friends have chores that they have to do in their homes?"

8. Blaming, Counterattacking, Judging

Most people will at times respond to the other's defensiveness or lack of cooperation by going on the attack. For example:

➤ "You never want to do what I suggest!"

➤ "You selfish brat! You apologize right now for what you said."

9. Withdrawing, Diverting, Trying to be Funny

When others become emotional, some people may respond by making a hasty retreat or trying to change the subject to something more comfortable or saying something funny to lighten the mood. Such responses are how we try to deal with our own discomfort with the situation. For example:

➤ "Okay. Let's forget the whole idea and go get some dinner."

➤ "You're right. I am a mean old slave driver and I bought a new whip today to keep you in line!"

Recognize any of these responses? Go back to the three negotiation scenarios presented earlier and read what you wrote in response to each one. Next to each of your answers, write down the numbers corresponding to the common responses just outlined that seem to fit your response. (It is easy to combine two or three categories in one response.)

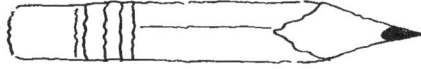

DOES YOUR RESPONSE CARRY A RISK?

You may be wondering if any of the nine common listening responses were the wrong thing to say or do in the earlier exercise with the three scenarios. Let's just say they can result in undesired reactions from the other person. You can probably figure out how that might happen.

For each category of response listed below, identify at least one way the response could result in a communication breakdown or unwanted reaction from the other person.

1. Telling, Commanding

_____

_____

2. Moralizing, Preaching, Expressing Shoulds and Oughts

_____

_____

3. Advising, Offering Suggestions

_____

_____

4. Complimenting, Praising, or Agreeing

_____

_____

5. Explaining, Being Logical

_____

_____

CONTINUED

6. Reassuring, Encouraging, Offering Sympathy

_____

_____

7. Asking Questions

_____

_____

8. Blaming, Counterattacking, Judging

_____

_____

9. Withdrawing, Diverting, Trying to Be Funny

_____

_____

Compare your answers with the authors' responses in the Appendix.

Using Active Listening

If you have checked the Appendix and learned the risks inherent in each of the common listening responses, you may be asking: How can I respond to others so they will be most likely to react positively and continue to communicate with me in an effective and productive way?

The answer is to use *active listening*. The following active listening responses are listed in order of effectiveness and level of skill required. Attentive Silence is the easiest and accomplishes the least and Verbal Restatement is the most challenging and accomplishes the most.

> **Attentive Silence**

> In contrast to passive silence, which is a form of withdrawal, attentive silence communicates attentiveness. You make good eye contact, look interested, assume an interested posture, and nod your head. Even though you say nothing, these behaviors create the impression that you are interested and listening. Does this prove to the other person that you have understood what she said? No. But it will be appreciated because it looks as if you are listening.

> **Attentive Words and Sounds**

> Making sounds or saying things such as "hmmm," "huh," "I see," "I hear you," and "I understand just what you mean" add to the impression of attentiveness. Do they prove to the other person that you have understood what he said? No. Your words and sounds do help, though, because now you look *and* sound attentive. Almost everyone responds positively to active listening forms 1 and 2 because they convey that you are interested and care about the other person.

> **Door-Openers or Prompts**

> This active listening technique is designed to help the other person open up and talk more. You can use either commands or questions to accomplish this. These are special commands and questions—different from common responses #1 (telling, commanding) and #7 (asking questions) discussed earlier. Examples of door-opener commands are *tell me more, please continue*, and *go on*. Knowing that some people do not like commands, you may prefer to use open-ended questions such as "What more do you want me to know?" "Then what happened?" "What are your thoughts on that?" "How will you proceed?" As a general rule, effective open-ended questions start with "what" or "how."

Both the commands and questions usually will result in the other person's opening up and talking more than he might normally because you seem to be genuinely interested and seem to really care. But do your prompts prove that you understood what she said in her original communication to you? No.

➤ **Verbal Restatement**

This is the only listening response that proves you really heard and understood what the other person just said to you. The idea is to say back to him what you think he just said to you without sounding like an echo or a parrot. It is important to paraphrase what the other person says rather than repeat it. What follows is a formula for verbal restatement that will be most likely to get a positive response and prove that you were really listening.

1. Paraphrase the content of the message. This proves you understood accurately.

2. Acknowledge the other person's feelings. This demonstrates empathy.

3. End with a "checkout question." This invites the other person to respond to what you just said.

Examples:

➤ The other person says to you, "My boss is driving me crazy with his poor time management and constant criticism!"

You respond, "You seem pretty unhappy with your boss. Right?"

➤ The other person says, "I just can't figure out what to do with this dumb thing! The instruction manual is useless and nothing seems to work!"

You respond, "Sounds like you're really frustrated with that thing. True?"

Active Listening for Understanding

Using all four active listening responses, including listening with empathy and understanding, can be almost magical. People almost always have a positive response when you communicate understanding and empathy. If they were feeling frustrated, angry, anxious, or otherwise emotional, you will notice that their emotions will level off. When you acknowledge good feelings such as excitement or pleasure, those good feelings will be reinforced and strengthened.

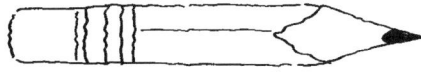

PRACTICE RESPONDING WITH EMPATHY

Like any new technique, verbal restatement requires practice to develop comfort and skill in using it. Try it in the following situations:

➤ The other person says, "I am at my wit's end! I'm putting in 10-hour days, taking work home on the weekends, and I still can't get caught up!"

You respond, _____

➤ The other person says to you, "Why are you so insensitive? I can't believe you told that blonde joke tonight with Joan and Emily standing right there!"

You respond, _____

➤ The other person says to you, "It seems that no matter how hard I try, my stepchildren just don't want to have anything to do with me."

You respond, _____

Compare your active listening responses with those of the authors in the Appendix.

Practice verbal restatement daily for several weeks. Use it a few minutes every day in conversations and you will quickly develop skill. Then you will be more likely to use it in situations when it is important to demonstrate empathy and understanding.

A P P E N D I X

Following Through with What You Have Learned

Achieving a balanced life is an ongoing process. It requires following through with what you have learned by reading and doing the exercises in this book. The suggestions below will help you maintain your success.

➤ Review this book tomorrow! Most people quickly forget most of what they just learned and a review within 24 hours will help you remember.

➤ Read the book again within two weeks and think about your answers to the exercises. Change some if they need changing. Write new goals and action steps as you think of them.

➤ Talk with someone about what you have learned. The ideas you share with others will be what you remember best. If you share your goals with others, you also increase the probability that these people will help you achieve them.

➤ Commit to reading at least two or three other books mentioned in this book. Check the Recommended Reading list at the end of this book.

➤ Listen to an audio program or watch a video program related to this topic. Complete an interactive computer-based learning program. Some of the titles in the Crisp series have videos and interactive learning programs.

➤ Take a course or training program relating to topics covered in this book.

➤ Review this book a third time in about one month.

➤ Reward yourself for following through and accomplishing your goals. Have a celebration!

Appendix to Part 2

Evaluate These Goal Statements

I will spend more time with my children. This is an activity rather than a result. What is the purpose of spending more time? What is this activity expected to achieve?

I will lose 12 pounds during the next four months. This is an effective goal statement—specific, measurable, achievable, with a time limit.

By the end of next year I will be able to have conversations in Spanish. This is a good goal statement.

I will retire comfortably by age 60. Even though this statement has a time limit, is stated as a result, and could be achievable if the time limit were realistic, it is vague. The statement could be improved by being more specific—defining the amount of capital or income rather than using the word comfortably.

I will work on improving my relationship with my spouse during the next year. This statement hints at a result but does not really define the desired outcome specifically. It also is somewhat vague about the time factor. Most important, it promises only effort (work on) rather than achievement.

I will have three new friends by the end of the summer. This goal statement fits the criteria for an effective goal.

Appendix to Part 3

Hear What You Say

The drivers in the example sentences are:

1. Please Others
2. Be Strong
3. Be Perfect
4. Hurry Up
5. Try Hard
6. Be Strong
7. Please Others
8. Be Perfect
9. Hurry Up
10. Try Hard

Seeing Your Drivers in Your Beliefs and Values

The way to succeed in work is to:

1. Be Perfect
2. Be Strong
3. Hurry Up
4. Try Hard
5. Please Others

In work and recreation it is best to:

1. Be Perfect
2. Please Others
3. Try Hard
4. Hurry Up
5. Be Strong

A good approach to decision-making is:

1. Please Others

2. Hurry Up

3. Try Hard

4. Be Perfect

5. Be Strong

In living life the following beliefs guide me:

1. Try Hard

2. Be Perfect

3. Be Strong

4. Please Others

5. Hurry Up

As a parent and/or a life partner, I should:

1. Please Others

2. Be Perfect

3. Be Strong

4. Hurry Up

5. Try Hard

Rethinking Your Underlying Messages

To replace "Be Perfect" messages:

➤ Relax, think, do it.

➤ Expect success!

➤ Set realistic goals. Allow plenty of time to achieve them.

➤ Work at a comfortable pace and do it well.

➤ Take pride in being able to do it easily.

➤ Success is achieving your goals.

To replace "Be Strong" messages:

➤ Be aware of feelings and share them.

➤ Have empathy and show you care.

➤ Practice win-win collaboration.

➤ It's okay to be scared. It's okay to take a chance.

➤ Trust others and let them be close.

➤ Courageous people share feelings with others.

To replace "Please Others" messages:

➤ I'm okay even when others disapprove.

➤ Be honest with others.

➤ My wants and needs are as important as those of others.

➤ You can show you care and allow others to do for themselves.

➤ It's okay to share anger, disappointment, and other negative feelings.

➤ It's okay to say no.

➤ My opinions and beliefs are valid. My rights are equal to those of others.

To replace "Try Hard" messages:

➤ Relax, think, do it.

➤ Expect success!

➤ Set realistic goals. Allow plenty of time to achieve them.

➤ Work at a comfortable pace and do it well.

➤ Take pride in being able to do it easily.

➤ Success is achieving your goals.

To replace "Hurry Up" messages:

➤ Take a breath. Think.

➤ Plan ahead. Set realistic goals and time limits.

➤ Let others go at their own pace and you will get better results.

➤ It's okay to relax. Stop and smell the roses!

➤ Allow others to speak without interruption.

➤ Listen to others and they will listen to you.

➤ Haste makes waste!

Changing Your Internal Dialogue

The following statements would be "allowing" responses:

"I would prefer to find someplace less expensive. Will you agree to that?"

"This is difficult! I may have to get some help."

[A challenge for people with high "Be Perfect" is to not correct others' inaccuracies. The best thing in this situation would be to say nothing!]

"Gosh! Look at the time. We may be a little late unless we leave now."

"I understand your frustration. We have all been putting in long hours since the layoffs and it is tiring, isn't it?"

Appendix to Part 5

Recognizing Behavior Styles

The statements reveal these behavior styles:

1. NAS
2. AG
3. AG
4. AS
5. NAS
6. AG
7. AS
8. NAS
9. NAS
10. AS

Communicating Assertively

Possible responses in the situations under "Practice Speaking Assertively" are:

"Honey, I really don't like making the vacation plans. Will you please do that while I catch up with work stuff so I will be able leave it behind and enjoy our vacation time together?"

"I appreciate your confidence in me and the generous offer you have made. I have evaluated the options thoroughly and decided that this opportunity does not fit with my values and priorities, so I am declining the offer. I hope you will understand and keep me in mind for other possibilities that would not require relocation."

Case Study: Adam Goes to College

1. Negotiating a clear, specific contract made a significant difference.

2. The contract between Adam and his parents met each of the contract requirements.

a. Yes, the contract was negotiated in an open conversation.

b. Adam's parents gained control over their finances and felt better about supporting their son in his pursuit of an education. Adam gained an incentive to manage his finances and get serious about his schoolwork and as a result also gained the satisfaction of earning his degree and graduating debt-free with better than a B average.

c. Yes, the commitments were realistic. Adam and his parents knew he should be able to control his finances and maintain at least a B average.

d. Yes, the contract was legal.

What Is a Valid Contract?

The first example is not a valid contract because there is no mutual agreement. The parent stopped negotiating and became demanding. This will result in the child's feeling forced. The child does not perceive a mutual benefit. As a result, the parent should expect a continuing battle around this issue.

The second example is a valid contract. The husband perceives the deal as mutually beneficial and accepts the offer.

Does Your Response Carry a Risk?

1. **Telling, Commanding.** Some people just do not like others telling them what to do and they will rebel, shut down, or withdraw in response. If the person does do what you tell him to do and it ends up being the wrong thing to do, then he may blame you. If it ends up being the right thing to do, he might come back to you the next time he has a problem and become increasingly dependent on you for guidance.

2. **Moralizing, Preaching, Expressing Shoulds and Oughts.** Some people may be highly offended if you try to impose your values on them by preaching to them or telling them what is best for them. They may argue in response to your pushing your beliefs. If they do what you tell them they *should*, then you have the same risks as explained above—blame or dependency.

3. **Advising, Offering Suggestions**. Many people will respond to advice by rejecting it, particularly if they did not ask for advice. Even if they did ask, they may still find fault with every word of advice you offer by saying, "Yes, but…" If they act on your advice you have the now familiar risks of their blaming you if it turns out to be bad advice or coming back for more if it was good advice.

4. **Complimenting, Praising, or Agreeing.** Even if your compliment or praise is sincere, some will hear it as insincere, phony flattery and will be offended. Others may interpret your kind words as telling them they are right and then they may make a bad decision. If you agree with them, they may also choose to take an unfortunate course of action and later blame you. If you agree with them or seem to be taking their side, they may mention to others that you agree, and then you could find yourself drawn into a situation in which you did not intend to become involved.

5. **Explaining, Being Logical.** This can come across as patronizing (even if you are trying to be helpful). This response can also communicate that you are discounting the importance of what the other person just shared with you. Because this response does not address the other person's emotions, she may feel that you have no empathy.

6. **Reassuring, Encouraging, Offering Sympathy.** Others may hear this response as insincere platitudes or as patronizing. Even if your supportive words help the other person feel better, you may have reduced the probability that he will take action on the problem. If he feels better as a result of your reassurances, he may be back every time he feels bad.

7. **Asking Questions to Get More Details, Information (also Yes or No Questions).** Some people will just stop talking instead of opening up because they are uncomfortable with your interrogation. If the other person does answer your questions, you are determining the subject of discussion, which may not be what she needs to be thinking about or what she intended to talk about (sidetrack). You can ask dozens of questions and still not understand the problem or not be successful in getting her to reveal the most significant thing (which may be something she doesn't want you to know!). Yes or no questions result in one-word responses, and both of you will become frustrated with that quickly. Finally, even if you ask all the right questions and identify and clarify the problem so it can be solved, you did all of the thinking and guess what will happen the next time the person has a problem? Right! She'll be back!

8. **Blaming, Counterattacking, Judging.** Many people automatically respond this way when the other person is emotional. This response usually will invite defensiveness from the other person and can escalate into a full-blown argument.

9. **Withdrawing, Diverting, Trying to be Funny.** Even saying nothing and hoping the other person will go away is a version of withdrawing. You may be uncomfortable with what the person has said and not want to get involved, so you try to escape as quickly as you can or change the subject. If your discomfort prompts you to say something designed to be funny, the other person may be offended. This response typically will communicate to the other person that you do not care.

Practice Responding with Empathy

Possible verbal restatements in the three situations are:

"You sound really frustrated with not being able to get caught up! Right?"

"You're pretty upset with me and you seem concerned that Joan and Emily may have been offended. Is that what you're saying?"

"You're really disappointed that you can't seem to connect with your stepchildren. Is that what you're feeling?"

Additional Reading

Bader, Ellyn, Peter Pearson, and Judith Schwartz. *Tell Me No Lies: How to Face the Truth and Build a Loving Marriage*. NY: Golden Books Adult Publishing, 2000.

Bonet, Diana. *The Business of Listening: A Practical Guide to Effective Listening*. Boston, MA: Thomson Learning/Course Technology, 2001.

Lakein, Alan. *How to Get Control of Your Time and Your Life*. Reissued NY: New American Library, 1996).

Lloyd, Sam. *Developing Positive Assertiveness*. Boston, MA: Thomson Learning/Course Technology, 2002.

Lloyd, Sam, and Tina Berthelot. *Self-Empowerment*. Boston, MA: Thomson Learning/Course Technology, 2003.

Manning, Marilyn and Patricia Haddock. *Developing as a Professional*. Boston, MA: Thomson Learning/Course Technology, 2004.

Merrill, A. Roger, and Rebecca Merrill. *Life Matters: Creating a Dynamic Balance of Work, Family, Time & Money*. NY: McGraw-Hill, 2003.

Pollar, Odette. *Surviving Information Overload*. Boston, MA: Thomson Learning/Course Technology, 2004.

Scott, Dru. *How to Put More Time in Your Life*. NY: Signet, 1981.

Steiner, Claude. *Scripts People Live: Transactional Analysis of Life Scripts*. Reprinted. NY: Grove Press, 1990.

NOTES

NOTES

NOTES

NOTES

Now Available From

THOMSON
COURSE TECHNOLOGY
™

Books • Videos • CD-ROMs • Computer-Based Training Products

Subject Areas Include:

Management
Human Resources
Communication Skills
Personal Development
Sales/Marketing
Finance
Coaching and Mentoring
Customer Service/Quality
Small Business and Entrepreneurship
Training
Life Planning
Writing

VERM